Dogs

John
Townsend

Editor: Nick Pierce

Published in Great Britain in MMXVII by
Book House, an imprint of
The Salariya Book Company Ltd
25 Marlborough Place, Brighton BN1 1UB

ISBN: 978-1-911242-94-9

1 3 5 7 9 8 6 4 2

A CIP catalogue record for this book is available
from the British Library.

Printed and bound in China.
Printed on paper from sustainable sources.

Illustrations by Suzanne Khushi, Leanne Morris,
Michael Richardson, Shutterstock, Anna Zakharchenko

Visit
www.salariya.com
for our online catalogue and
free fun stuff.

Dogs

John Townsend

BOOK HOUSE
a SALARIYA imprint

'Dogs are born with a unique instinct; to lick, love and laud the hand that feeds them.'

Contents

Introduction

A dog is like...

- An adorably trusting toddler... but without the tantrums

- An adorably turbulent teenager... but without the tantrums

- An adorably playful partner... but without the... (choose your own ending!)

If you want a friend, get a dog.

Not only will your pet be your constant companion, but also (according to the British Psychological Society), walking with a dog at least triples the number of social interactions a person has. Dogs elicit positive social contact even when the animal looks fierce or the owner is particularly scruffy and unattractive!

According to some...

- If your dog is fat, you're not getting enough exercise.

- My goal in life is to be as good a person as my dog already thinks I am.

- Children are for people who can't have dogs.

- If aliens saw us walking our dogs and picking up their poop, who would they think is in charge?

- The reason a dog has so many friends is that he wags his tail instead of his tongue.

- You have to feel sorry for people who don't have dogs. They have to pick up food they drop on the floor.

Introduction

Criticise dog-lovers and they'll shrug indifferently; criticise their dogs and they'll bite.

'Quo me amat, amat et canem meam.'
'Qui aime Pertrand, aime son chien.'
'Quién bién quiérs a beliram, bien quiére a su can.'
'Love me, love my dog.'

No other domestic animal on the planet comes in so many shapes, sizes and varieties as dogs, with the unique ability to connect with humans through exceptional intelligence. A world without dogs is almost unimaginable, and doubtless unbearable for millions of us. With the bond between humans and dogs having developed over thousands of years, canines have been moulded more than any other species to become 'man's best friend'. Embrace them or avoid them, you'll surely be amazed at the impact dogs have on all of us – and we on them.

9

Despite frightening annual statistics of dog bites, attacks and resulting cynophobia, our love affair with dogs continues to deepen. With well over 525 million dogs worldwide, their numbers keep growing; a quarter of British and US households now own pet dogs as beloved family members. Pooch pampering and all things dog, in the US especially, is massive business – yet in some countries stray canines are considered to be pariahs and a major risk to human health and safety.

Lovable dogs are loved; fearful dogs are feared. No surprise there. You could say the same for any species, including humans. But it is the subject of dogs, probably more than any other animal, that seems to produce the strongest feelings in us. Depending on our own experiences and personal encounters, we will either hug them unashamedly or recoil.

Dogs, but more especially their owners, so often divide us. We either go weak at the knees at a cute puppy in advertisements for bathroom tissue, marvel at the dedicated concentration of guide dogs, sheep dogs and sniffer dogs as they perform wonders, or we curse the state of pavements, that snarling dogfight in the park or the latest child-mauling savage in the news. But of course, dogs, like children, tend to behave according to how they are treated and raised. Blaming dogs for the sins of their masters is like accusing the victims of crimes for perpetrating them. Dogs, after all, are by and large our own creation – with a little help from a few genetic raw materials.

Whether your dog is seen as a cuddly chum, a working companion or just another member of the family, the wolf within has potential to stir. Although we may smother pets with sentimentality loaded with human virtues and qualities, dogs are very much rooted in the wild, with deep-seated primordial instincts. Despite all those anthropomorphic myths, legends, inspiring narratives, films and video clips, the science and history of dogs reveals an ongoing battle between nature and nurture – as you are about to discover...

Chapter 1
Dogs: A brief history

'If it could be shown that the greyhound, bloodhound, terrier, spaniel and bulldog, which we all know propagate their kind truly, were the offspring of any single species, then such facts would have great weight in making us doubt about the immutability of the many closely allied natural species...'

Charles Darwin,
***On the Origin Of Species*, 1859**

Can the Chihuahua and Saint Bernard really belong to the same species? Surely Darwin wasn't seriously suggesting that all dogs shared the same ancestors. Outrageous though his claim once seemed, nearly 140 years later he was proved correct. In 1997, geneticists analysing canine DNA were able to conclude that all dogs, whether big, small, smooth, hairy, sleek or stocky were descended from grey wolves (canis lupus).

The finer details of dog evolution are somewhat convoluted – suffice it to say that wolves descended from weasel-like carnivores called Miacids that lived over 40 million years ago. Around 6 million years ago, a branch of these predators had evolved into 'canis', the ancestors of wolves, coyotes, jackals and other wild dogs – their fossil remains having been found in Asia, Europe and Africa. By about 1.8 million years ago, 'canis' animals were becoming more like today's wolves, which eventually spread through North America around 150,000 to 100,000 years ago. From the Neolithic Age to the Middle Ages (over 12,000 years), the grey wolf was the most widespread predator on Earth. It now only survives in the more remote northern regions of Europe, Asia and North America, having become extinct across most of Western Europe, Mexico and much of the USA. Their original worldwide range has reduced by about one-third.

Possibly as long as 100,000 years ago, the grey wolf began to take an interest in our human ancestors by prowling around their campsites (no villages yet), trying to snatch something to eat. Doubtless they were first seen as dangerous pests and chased off, until their uses were put to the test – such as catching vermin or guarding the camp. Wolf cubs with gentler natures may have been reared to become reasonably tame, but the oldest archaeological evidence for a domestic dog-like animal comes later, from around 33,000 years ago. In 2010 a fossil skull of 'Razbo' was excavated in Siberia, which is thought to be from one of the earliest domesticated dogs of human hunter-gatherers.

As domesticated wolves became tamer, they kept campsites free of rubbish, vermin and therefore disease. People who lived in these cleaner campsites grew up stronger than people who shooed wolves away. Eventually, the 'dog-lovers' became established all over the world, with their canine pets evolving to digest cooked and grain-based food.

At some point, people began to teach canines to obey them, and do work such as pull sledges. It is uncertain whether this domestication of dogs happened only once, in one place, or many times over Europe and Asia, but all known dogs today around the world are descended from Central Asian dogs of about 13,000 BC. Such dogs would have been scavengers, rather than be fed directly. In fact, even today, about three out of four dogs around the world live on their own around human dwellings, having to find their own food.

So, as civilisations developed, tamed wolves changed in body and temperament. Their skulls, teeth and paws shrank, their ears flopped and they appeared more 'doggy'. Over thousands of years, dogs have mated with each other, cross-bred with wild dogs, travelled over the world, and been repeatedly selectively bred by humans. The resulting ebb and flow of genes has turned dog evolution into something of a genetic soup. Enough to say, the animals with a more docile disposition have been deliberately bred to create more responsive and obedient pets – even able to read the expressions and signals from human faces. The savage wolf eventually turned into a loyal dog – with many of today's breeds showing little resemblance to their forebears. At least, not on the outside!

'The hour between dog and wolf, that is, dusk, when the two can't be distinguished from each other, suggests a lot of other things besides the time of day…The hour in which…every being becomes his own shadow, and thus something other than himself.'

Jean Genet

The rest is history

Dogs have played their part in the evolution of human civilisations. They have accompanied soldiers into action since at least the time of the Roman Empire. Apparently Alexander the Great's dog, Peritas, fearlessly bit a charging elephant (part of the attacking Persian army) thereby saving his world-conquering master. So dogs have shaped our past, just as we have shaped theirs.

The dachshund is one of the oldest breeds, going all the way back to ancient Egypt. One of its earliest uses was to hunt badgers. Greyhounds were also bred in ancient Egypt some 5,000 years ago. They arrived in Britain over 1,000 years ago and were used by the Saxons to hunt hares. Pekinese dogs, also one of the oldest breeds, were sacred to the emperors of China for 2,000 years.

18

A dog was blamed for changing the course of British history when Cardinal Wolsey, acting as an emissary of Henry VIII, took his dog Urian with him to an important meeting with Pope Clement VII. The Cardinal's mission was to ask the pope to annul the king's marriage to Catherine of Aragon. During the meeting, Urian happened to bite the pope. The angered pontiff thus refused to grant the annulment. The only divorce that came from this meeting was the one between England and the Roman Church. Dogs undoubtedly have much to answer for!

Woof
Woof

Chapter 2
Canine behaviour

'If a dog will not come to you after having looked you in the face, you should go home and examine your conscience.'

Woodrow Wilson

*U*nlike their wolf ancestors, which only breed once a year in the wild, domestic dogs can have two litters a year, a typical pregnancy lasting 63 days. The resulting puppies (a general average being seven in a litter) will soon display instinctive behaviour patterns – but firstly we take a peep into the private world of the puppy.

Puppies' eyes (always blue) open after around 12 days. At around the same time, their ears – which are flat to the side of their heads at first – begin to grow large and floppy or stand up in a 'pricked' position, depending on the breed. The channel leading from the outer ear to the eardrum also begins to open, and, for the first time, puppies can hear.

Puppies' milk teeth begin to break through their gums at 4 weeks after birth. By the time they are 6 weeks old, they can eat solid food. Many breeders let pups move to a new home at 10–12 weeks (and many mother dogs are relieved to see them go). However, unlike wolves, young dogs are able to transfer their puppy affections to new humans until they are 4 months old or more. By that time their eyes will usually have turned brown, the normal adult colour. At 4 months, puppies begin to grow adult teeth, and lose their baby ones.

The age at which dogs become fully grown varies from around 9–12 months for toy dogs to 18 months for larger ones. The average dog's lifespan is around 13 years, if they are lucky. But larger dogs often have shorter lives, and smaller dogs can live for much longer. Growing quickly puts stress on a large dog's bones and muscles. So do years of moving a big, heavy body around. Scientists also suggest that, in order to grow so big so quickly, large dogs are genetically programmed with 'speeded up' development. Genes for extra-fast growth also make it likely that a big dog will develop diseases of old age while still quite young.

It is often said that we can calculate how old a dog would be in human years by multiplying its age by 7. This is not strictly true. Not only do big dogs age faster than small ones, but all dogs develop at a different rate from humans. In particular, they mature much more quickly. For example, a one-year-old dog from a small to medium breed is at about the same stage in its life-cycle as a teenage human.

How to read a dog's body language

Decoding a dog's posture, face, sounds and tail movements can help forewarn if an unfamiliar dog is friend or foe. It is worth considering the more obvious signals a dog might be giving, before suggesting what appropriate action to take, should man's best friend turn out not to be so!

Get up close and personal with your nearest friendly canine, and you will observe a wide range of movements and expressions. All have evolved to signal the dog's state of mind, and its intentions:

Eyes

• Eyes open normally = alert, playful

• Eyes wide open = excited, friendly

• Eyes wide open, watchful = on guard

• Eyes wide open, following
  movements = chasing

• Eyes slightly narrowed = anxious

- Eyes narrowed, head turned away = fearful, avoiding conflict

- Eyes narrowed, 'whale eye' (white showing) = submissive, ready to run away

- Eyes wide open, whale eye = stressed

- Eyes narrowed, staring and glaring = aggressive – watch out!

Ears

- Ears pricked up, facing forward, relaxed = playful

- Ears pricked up, forward, perky = excited, chasing, on guard

- Ears pricked up, turned to catch sound = alert, chasing

- Ears pricked up, standing tall = dominant

- Ears pushed forward, stiffly = aggressive

- Ears flat against head = aggression or fear (depending on posture, mouth and teeth)

25

- Ears tilted backwards = anxious, submissive, ready to run away

Mouth

- Mouth open, teeth 'smiling' (relaxed) = friendly

- Mouth open, teeth part-covered = playful

- Mouth open, teeth visible, panting = excited, chasing

- Mouth closed or slightly open, no teeth showing = alert

- Snarling, growling, fangs bared = aggressive

- Snarling, snapping teeth = on guard

- Lips 'grinning' (tight and tense) = anxious, submissive

- Teeth bared, drooling = fearful, ready to run away

Posture

- Posture alert, weight balanced on four paws = happy, normal

- Posture tense, leaning forwards, hackles (hair on back of neck) raised = aggression

- Posture tense, standing tall = guarding

- Posture stiff, body low, ready to spring = chasing

- Posture tense, back lowered, shivering = anxious, fearful, ready to run away

- Standing still or wriggling rear end = friendly

- Wriggling, bouncing, fast pacing = excited

- Play bow, bouncing, jumping, circling = playful

- On back, belly up, front paw raised = submission

- Licking nose = peaceful gesture, reducing stress

- Turning head away = avoiding conflict

- Turning back on = avoiding conflict

- Trapped in corner = BEWARE. An angry or frightened dog may attack first, think later. Or not think at all.

Tail

- Tail up, wagging = alert, friendly, excited

- Tail wagging wildly = playful

- Tail straight out behind, fairly low = chasing

- Tail straight or raised, perhaps fluffed up = aggression

- Tail stiff, straight behind = guarding

- Tail partly down = anxious

- Tail between legs = fear, submission, ready to run away

Dealing with a hostile dog

Anyone delivering letters or goods to homes will presumably encounter the occasional unfriendly dog, particularly if it sees its job as guarding the property. If a dog runs up to you, snarls and primes itself to lunge, conventional advice is to stay calm and take a few measures to diffuse the situation.

Apparently, there's some truth to the old adage that dogs can 'sense fear'. If you panic, run or scream, you may make a dog feel more confident to attack, or you may actually appear threatening. If a snarling dog approaches, it is advisable to stand completely still with your hands at your sides, rigid and motionless, while averting your eyes. In many cases a dog will lose interest and walk away if ignored.

Don't...

- Don't wave your arms or kick out as the dog may perceive these actions as threatening.

- Don't make eye contact, since that could also cause the dog to lunge. Stand sideways to the dog and keep it in peripheral vision instead of facing it. This will signal to the dog that you are not a threat.

• Don't open your hands but keep fingers curled into fists to avoid getting them bitten. The dog may come close, even sniffing you, without actually biting.

• Don't try to run away. Running can awaken the dog's prey instinct to chase. It may pursue you vigorously even if its initial intent was playful. Besides, you won't outrun a dog!

If things are still getting scary... facing the dog and commanding it to 'leave' can show you are in control. By using a strong, deep, confident command while still avoiding direct eye contact, you may intimidate the dog to back off.

According to the handbooks, once a dog loses interest in you, it is preferable to leave the scene slowly by backing away without sudden movements. Staying calm and quiet can be a test of your nerves, but the experts recommend it's the best thing to do as long as the dog isn't actually biting you.

Like children, some dogs are brought up not to fight, while others have their aggression encouraged, either purposely or through error. When another dog off its lead attacks your pet dog who is doing no harm to anyone and is on a lead, what can you do?

Experts tell us that dogs initiate fighting when they feel insecure around other dogs. It is worth remembering some key aspects of dog behaviour when taking Fido for a stroll in the park.

• Dogs may display aggression to other dogs approaching them outside, especially when their owner gets tense and yanks on the lead. Try not to tense up with the lead or yell during the approach of another dog. That can make your dog associate the sight of another dog with punishment or anxiety.

• Dogs growl at younger dogs in an attempt to put youngsters in their place, so this needn't be a sign of imminent attack.

• When dogs growl at younger dogs, this leads to the development of active appeasement on the part of the lower-ranking dog. The lower-ranking dog learns to show deference, which signals that he understands and respects the hierarchy. Usually the older/more dominant dog will then let the youngster play.

- Playing is more than just having fun for dogs; it's a way to compete and a way to establish rank, rather than trying to cause each other harm.

Without dwelling on the potential dangers from dogs (and before going on to revel in their positive brain power), it is worth mentioning that, although any dog has the potential to 'release the wolf within', certain breeds seem more hard-wired to become aggressive. This list is probably as expected – as ranked by the USA's Centers for Disease Control and Prevention – for the breeds implicated in a majority of dog-bite fatalities:

- Pit bulls
- Rottweilers
- German shepherds
- Huskies
- Wolf hybrids
- Malamutes
- Doberman pinschers
- Chow-chows

- Saint Bernards
- Great Danes

Of course, this isn't to say smaller breeds are necessarily less aggressive, just that they are less powerful and so less likely to cause major injury. But fear not, should you feel all dogs have been tarred by the same violent brush... from here on, man's best friend receives much more of a pat on the back and a whistle of approval. The wolf will be left behind.

Bark

'When it comes to dog-training, it's very easy. Your dog will soon train you to throw a stick, shake his paw or provide food whenever he wants.'

34

Chapter 3
Canine intelligence

'Intelligence is based on how efficient a species became at doing the things they need to survive.'

Charles Darwin

*D*ogs are clever – most dog owners will happily tell you so and recount tales to demonstrate the impressive thinking, reasoning, puzzle-solving, memory and maybe even emotions of their faithful pet. Up there with dolphins, primates and cats, we tend to place dogs among the most intelligent species after humans. But is that really justified?

Given that defining, let alone attempting to measure intelligence in any species is something of a hit and miss affair, it's nonetheless worth trying to put the canine brain under the microscope. There might just be a few answers to some of those questions about dog psychology.

So far, most research comparing cat and dog cognition has confirmed what many pet owners already assume: dogs are generally attentive and responsive because they want praise; cats, by and large, don't care what you want, and they don't particularly want your help, thank you. Despite all the exceptions, are these realistic stereotypes? In a nutshell, in terms of the ratio of brain mass to body mass, a dog's brain takes up 1.2% of total body mass. Humans' brains occupy about 2% of total body mass, and cats' brains occupy about 0.9%. Yet when it comes to intelligence, brain size alone isn't necessarily a major factor, as brain morphology and functioning are far more complex. The usual conclusions of studies (if cats can be persuaded to participate in the first place) show that dogs more often demonstrate a higher social IQ than cats, while cats can sometimes solve harder cognitive problems – but only if they're in the mood. Dogs are likely to attempt anything to please you if there's a biscuit involved!

You can try out a simple 'dognition' test on your own pet dog by observing any copying behaviour. Most dogs learn by watching how another dog or person solves a problem and they simply do the same. Some can copy types of body language – called 'emotional contagion'. For example, if humans see, hear, or think about someone yawning, they often feel an irresistible urge to yawn as well. Contagious yawning is related to empathy scores in adults – but it seems some dogs also contagiously yawn. So try a big yawn in front of your dog and see if it yawns back. If it does, this may well demonstrate your dog's level of emotional contagion... or just that it's tired of you carrying out psychological experiments!

But here's the bombshell, as reported in *Scientific American* in 2013, under the title '*The Brilliance of the Dog Mind: New science reveals the multiple intelligences of mankind's best friend.*' The report states that 'There are several measures, like contagious yawning, that show that dogs probably at least have a basic form of empathy (human infants who do not contagiously yawn typically have low empathy scores). And there are studies showing that dogs and humans experience a rise in oxytocin, the 'hug hormone'

when we hug and pet them (although it seems dogs get a higher boost in oxytocin when they are petted by women, as opposed to men!). Make of that what you will.

So, it seems both humans and dogs thrive on hugs, love and attention. Giving your dog plenty of love and attention is obviously an important part of raising a happy pet, yet studies in dog psychology show this alone won't raise an emotionally and mentally healthy dog. Dogs apparently need a healthy balance of affection, attention and discipline in order to feel secure, safe and happy. Hardly rocket science, but we all know dog owners who are ruled by their dogs rather than vice versa, simply due to lack of discipline.

Various research indicates that many dogs have intelligence and understanding on a par with a human toddler of about two years old, in that they have the capacity to learn how to count (or at least recognise different amounts) and even understand up to 150 words. While their vocabulary may never reach the complexity of a toddler's, dogs can easily understand a wide range of vocal tones. For example, dogs may understand their name and react when called, but the tone of voice used when calling can change their behaviour when they come running. Happy tones make a dog excited and playful, while angry tones make dogs feel sad or frightened. If there is fear in your voice, a dog may think you're being threatened and rush to protect you. So it seems how you talk to your dog can be more significant than what you actually say.

Emotional Intelligence

Many dog owners are notorious for their firm belief that Fido understands their every word and shares the whole range of human feelings. While dogs obviously experience basic emotions like happiness, fear and sadness, what about more complicated feelings? Studies show that dogs do show signs of experiencing jealousy, though not exactly how we experience it.

Researchers put dogs side by side and gave them commands. Both dogs would perform the same command yet only one would get a treat. The one not given a treat showed signs of agitation, avoided contact with the rewarded dog and scratched more often. This was attributed to jealousy, as these signs of agitation appeared more frequently in the experiment with pairs of dogs than in times when a dog was alone and refused a reward.

Interestingly, if one dog is being given something special as a treat such as a piece of steak, while another is given something plain like a biscuit, there are no signs of jealousy. Dogs seem only to care that they actually get rewarded, not what the reward is. Try that with children and compare the results!

Many a dog owner has entered a room only to find something torn to shreds or a little deposit on the new carpet – with the furry culprit staring up with a sad expression. It's easy to believe that this is the dog expressing remorse, but apparently guilt is not technically part of the canine emotional repertoire. When a dog sees the look of disapproval on an owner's face or hears anger or disappointment in the voice, it reacts negatively with expressions suggesting sadness. Yet dogs are unlikely to associate being reprimanded with their previous action, now forgotten, and simply look sad from being spoken to sharply rather than from actually feeling guilty.

In experiments, dogs tend to react the same way no matter if they performed the crime or not. Merely seeing or hearing the negativity from their owners, or anticipating punishment, is enough to bring on that sad puppy-dog face. There again, if you are one of those dog-lovers who is convinced your beloved hound is not only super intelligent, forever understanding and on your emotional wavelength entirely, you may well dismiss findings from dog psychologists or the growing number of canine psychiatrists offering to re-programme dog brains. Instead, you may wish to glimpse some of the surprising findings from the following scientific research into what other secrets your dog may be hiding, as further canine revelations unfold...

Woof

The frequent excuse for why I failed science at school was; 'The dog ate my homework'. The dog is now a professor of microbiology.

Chapter 4
Dogs and science

'I'm not sure if I was the first man in space or the last dog.'

Yuri Gagarin

Dogs

Scientists have long been interested in studying dogs, probably because their subjects are often so willing to please. If your own dog dribbles on your feet the minute you walk in the room, it either associates your appearance with food or it is reminding you of the famous experiments conducted by Ivan Pavlov in 1901 to show how dogs (and many of us, no doubt) can be conditioned to respond to certain signals.

Noting how dogs salivated at the sight of food, Pavlov rang a bell as a stimulus whenever he gave food to his dogs. After a number of repetitions, he tried the bell without food. As expected, the bell on its own now caused an increase in salivation, proving the dogs had learned an association between the bell and the food. Because this response was learned (or conditioned), it is called a conditioned response. Pavlov's dogs became famous in the scientific world for demonstrating a type of learned behaviour. Likewise, if you respond to a bark by instantly reaching for the lead, your dog has conditioned you to respond through an unconscious learned reflex. Dogs seem to have learned a lot from Pavlov!

Russian war-time scientists

One of the hideous ideas of Stalin's scientists in World War 2 was to deploy 'canine killers' against Nazi tanks. Kamikaze dogs fitted with explosives were taught to carry them to the advancing enemy tanks. The dogs were trained to go under the tanks where handles sticking up from their backs would catch and detonate the explosives. To train them to do this, the dogs were kept without food, then released as hot food was put under tanks. The dogs soon learned, Pavlov-style, to associate tanks with food. The problem came when the Nazi tanks arrived, smelling different from the diesel Russian tanks. As such, some of the dogs ran back to shelter under the more familiar Russian tanks and blew those up instead. The project was a failure.

Russian astronomy

During the 1950s and 1960s the USSR used dogs in space rockets to determine whether human spaceflight was possible. Scientists monitored at least 57 missions using passenger dogs. Most survived; the few that died were lost mostly through technical failures. One exception was Laika, a stray dog from the streets of

Moscow, trained for the Soviet space program in 1957. She was selected as the sole occupant of Sputnik 2, becoming the first animal to orbit Earth. At the time, the technology didn't exist to de-orbit the spacecraft and return it to Earth safely, so Soviet officials announced that Laika was euthanized humanely just before the oxygen ran out on the sixth day of orbit. It was not until 45 years later that it was admitted the dog actually died within hours of launch, due to overheating. In 2008, a small monument to Laika was erected near the military research base where she was trained.

Good for you

In 2003, scientists reported the results of long-term studies that tried to find out whether pet owners led happier, healthier lives than people without pets. Over 11,000 respondents took part, from Australia, China, Germany and other lands. The results were surprising, even to dog-lovers:

- People with pets were healthier than people without them.

- Pet-owners made almost 20% fewer visits to their doctors.

- Stroking a cat or dog slowed heartbeats and lowered blood-pressure; in other words, it reduced stress.

- Patients with a serious illness were more likely to recover if they had a pet.

In the UK, similar studies showed that:

- Children with pets are less likely to take time off school.

- Children with cats or dogs are less likely to suffer from hay fever, asthma or animal allergies.

Colour vision

It was only in 2013 that Russian scientists disproved the myth that dogs can only see in black and white. For decades, scientists believed dogs could see just in monochrome and were only able to distinguish between objects visually by how light or dark they looked. But after a study at the University of Washington that showed dogs could actually distinguish between certain colour shades, Russian scientists took things further. They proved that not only do dogs have a limited colour range, but they also use this visual spectrum to select different coloured objects from a line-up.

Previously, dog trainers would avoid using coloured objects when training pets, but these findings should improve how dogs are trained and what they are capable of learning. So maybe Fido does prefer you in that blue hat rather than the yellow, after all. However, to a dog, orange, red and green all appear to be the same brownish-yellow colour. Even though a bright orange ball may be visible to a human, to a dog it blends in with the grass. The best colour for dog toys appears to be purple or blue and white. You can now go ahead and conduct your own research into which combination of colours and patterns your dog sees best.

Do cats and dogs really love us?

Small-scale scientific studies in 2016 analysed the oxytocin hormone that we and dogs release when we interact. We humans produce the hormone in our brains when we care about someone. When we see a loved one, the levels in our bloodstream typically rise by 40-60%. Neuroscientist, Dr Paul Zak checked the oxytocin levels in both cats and dogs after they had spent time playing with their owners.

He took saliva samples from 10 cats and 10 dogs on two occasions – 10 minutes before a playtime session with their owners and immediately afterwards – testing both samples for oxytocin. The results showed that the hormone increased by an average of 57.2% in dogs but only by 12% in cats. So, in theory, this suggests that dogs love their owners more than cats do! That must make it official – your dog really does love to be with you, whereas the cat may take more convincing. Science will doubtless try to tell us why in due course.

Arf
Arf

Chapter 5
Folklore and superstition

Cave tibi cane muto, aqua silente
Beware of a silent dog and still water
(The Romans warned that stagnant water is likely to poison, while a silent dog is likely to bite)

Dogs

Old myths, legends and nursery tales are steeped in all things canine; heroic hounds or evil dogs, wolves and werewolves. From the earliest folktales, dogs have been credited with the power of sensing the supernatural and any being invisible to human eyes.

In ancient Persia, dogs were believed to protect the dying soul from possession by evil spirits. When a person was dying, a dog was stationed by the bedside to keep away the negative spirits that hovered near newly released souls.

Hecate was the ancient Greek goddess of magic, witchcraft and the night. She was represented as dog-shaped or was accompanied by a dog – and her approach was heralded by howling. As if such a canine character didn't scare the Greeks enough, there was always the dreaded Cerberus, often called the 'Hound of Hades', the monstrous multi-headed dog, who guarded the gates of the underworld, preventing the dead from leaving. Dogs didn't get a good press back then.

According to Welsh folklore, the hounds of Annwn growled loudest when they were far away, and as they drew nearer, they became softer and more sinister. Their coming was seen as a portent of death. It is also in Wales that the grave of a heroic dog of legend can still be found. The story of Gelert, that most faithful of hounds, is told on the famous tombstone at Beddgelert:

'In the 13th century Llewelyn, prince of North Wales, had a palace at Beddgelert. One day he went hunting without Gelert, 'The Faithful Hound', who was unaccountably absent. On Llewelyn's return the truant, stained and smeared with blood, joyfully sprang to meet his master. The prince alarmed hastened to find his son, and saw the infant's cot empty, the bedclothes and floor covered with blood. The frantic father plunged his sword into the hound's side, thinking it had killed his heir. The dog's dying yell was answered by a child's cry. Llewelyn searched and discovered his boy unharmed, but nearby lay the body of a mighty wolf which Gelert had slain. The prince filled with remorse is said never to have smiled again. He buried Gelert here'.

Good luck – and living ghosts

On the whole, dogs are sensible, down-to-earth creatures, so perhaps it's not surprising that there are relatively few superstitions connected with them, compared with spookier, flightier creatures such as cats and birds. But a few have survived. Like most other folk beliefs, they deal with matters of everyday importance: the weather, the difficulties of life, romance and death.

- It's unlucky to meet a barking dog early in the morning.

- Being followed by a strange dog will bring good luck – or is terribly unlucky. (It all depends where you live.)

- A strange dog calling at your house means that you will meet a new friend.

- A howling dog means that death is approaching.

- A dog with seven toes can see ghosts.

- A barking dog on St Andrew's Day (30

November) tells young girls where their husbands will come from.

- Three white dogs seen together (a very unusual occurrence) are lucky.

- A black dog (very widespread) is a sign of evil.

- A dog barking after midnight is seeing the ghosts of living people who will die soon.

- If your dog refuses to follow you, it's a sign that something bad will soon be coming your way.

- A dog eating grass foretells rain.

- Plans made while sitting near a dog-rose bush will always fail.

- To bring good fortune in the New Year, feed a dog with bread and then push it out of the house. It will take any bad luck away with it.

Ten Old Proverbs of Canine Wisdom

- To live long, eat like a cat, drink like a dog. (Germany)

- Only mad dogs and Englishmen go out in the noonday sun. (India)

- Those who sleep with dogs will rise with fleas. (Italy)

- If you are a host to your guest, be a host to his dog also. (Russia)

- A house without either a cat or a dog is the house of a scoundrel. (Portugal)

Folklore and superstition

- An honest man is not the worse because a dog barks at him. (Denmark)

- Every dog is allowed one bite. (USA)

- A good dog deserves a good bone. (USA)

- If you stop every time a dog barks, your road will never end. (Saudi Arabia)

- Three things it is best to avoid: a strange dog, a flood, and a man who thinks he is wise. (Wales)

Tales to make you weep

Down the years, stories of dogs' devotion to their owners have been told, retold and doubtless corrupted, but their power to move us continues. Though the finer details may have changed in the various versions of these old stories, they are nonetheless based on true characters and real events. Although a book could be filled with accounts of heroic dogs and their loyalty, two in particular are world famous – and the third may be a folktale of the future (or even a rock musical!).

Greyfriars Bobby

No account of hero dogs could be complete without a mention of Greyfriars Bobby – a small but devoted Skye Terrier who used to accompany his owner, Auld Jock Gray, into Edinburgh – until, in 1858, Jock died. Jock's body was buried in the Greyfriars kirkyard in Edinburgh. It was strictly out of bounds to dogs, but Bobby was determined to be with his master. Although repeated efforts were made to drive Bobby away, he was eventually given permission to stay close to his master's grave. Bobby spent 14 years at Greyfriars; thousands came to see him, including Queen Victoria. He died in 1872, and a statue was erected to his memory the following year.

Hachiko

Strange but true, from 1925 to 1934, Bobby's story – or something very similar – was re-enacted in Japan. Hachiko, a golden-brown Akita, was in the habit of waiting for his master at the train station every day, when he returned from work. After his master died, Hachiko refused to change his behaviour, but continued going to the station every day, until his own death nine years later.

Masha

A 21st century Hachiko became a big news story in 2014. Masha, resembling a dachshund, arrived at reception at the hospital in Koltsovo, Russia every day for two years after her elderly owner was admitted. He was a pensioner from several kilometres away, who became ill and had turned up with his pet. Whilst he was staying on the ward, Masha was his only visitor and she trotted back home each evening to guard the house before returning to the hospital the next morning. When her owner died just before Christmas, the loyal dog continued to turn up every day, perhaps because she now had nowhere to live, or because she believed her master was still at the hospital.

Masha became a well-known and much loved figure at the hospital, where patients and workers ensured she had a warm bed and food to eat. When her story was featured in the *Siberian Times*, staff were inundated with requests from around the world from people desperate to adopt her and give her a home. Initially, the hospital had been keen to help find Masha a loving family to take care of her. But then came the announcement at Christmas.

'The little dog that has waited in vain at the same spot for the owner who has already died has finally been given a permanent home – in the very hospital where she has patiently sat for the past 12 months.'

Masha now had her own bed, the devoted attention of staff and patients each day... and fame. Time to pass the tissues?

Dog Years

Should you happen to be particularly honest, amiable and loyal, you may have been born in a certain year. With 2018 as The Chinese Year of the Dog, watch out for babies born then...

Bark

Chapter 6
Canine superpowers

They say my Afghan hound is a genius because she can play the trombone.
She's not at all. Little do they know she can't read a single note of music.

When it comes to special abilities, there is little doubt that dogs outshine us with their sense of hearing and smell. But are there other ways in which dogs have the upper paw? Many a dog owner will swear to some kind of extra sense at work in their beloved pet now and again. That said, it could just be that Fido's apparent 'extra sensory perception' is simply down to those other senses being especially amazing.

Super hearing

Dogs can hear in frequencies ranging from around 40 Hz to 60 kHz, depending on the breed and age. (Humans can hear in frequencies ranging from around 12 Hz to 20 kHz.) Dogs have more than 18 muscles that enable them to move their ears so they can precisely locate a sound. They can hear things up to four times further away than we can. While human ears are flat against the head, dogs' larger ears on the top are able to prick-up and pinpoint a noise. Dogs with erect ears can hear better than dogs with floppy or very hairy ears. With such acute hearing, dogs need to be able to filter out sounds, so they can often sleep through blaring music but jump up at the slightest rustle of the treats bag.

Sight

Being descended from twilight hunters, dogs have a section of their eye called the tapetum lucidum, which enables them to see well in low light. It's that reflective eye-shine you can see when light reflects in their eyes in the dark. Dogs can see motion better than we can – able to differentiate between their owners from distances of up to 900 metres (500 metres when their owners are stationary). Yet, given our superior colour vision, we have much better visual clarity than dogs. However, being able to see in ultraviolet, dogs notice certain things differently from us. Urine trails become visible to them in ultraviolet. Since urine is used by dogs to learn something about other dogs, it can be useful for them to see patches before giving them a good sniff (what some observers call 'reading their pee-mail').

Super smell

This supreme canine sense is all down to the brain's olfactory cortex, which is forty times bigger in dogs than it is in humans and many thousands of times more sensitive. The human nose can sense from about 4,000 to 10,000 different smells, and dogs around 30,000 to 100,000. To put all this in perspective of eyesight, it would be like you being able to see a third of a mile straight ahead and your dog seeing 3,000 miles beyond, just as clearly. In short, dogs are in a different league – with bloodhounds in a league of their own, given their approximately 230 million olfactory cells (scent receptors). Whereas our olfactory centre is about the size of a postage stamp, a bloodhound's can be as large as a handkerchief. As such, their incredible ability to pick up a cold trail has sent them on many fruitful police missions, following tracks over 300 hours old.

Other trained dogs have performed wonders in sniffing out everything from truffles, money and explosives to human remains, drugs and even bedbugs. Dogs are increasingly being used in medicine for detecting illness in humans, or warning of an oncoming epileptic seizure in their owner. It seems that dogs can smell changes in our body due to cancer and other biological conditions.

Extra powers

After natural disasters, stories often emerge about people who were warned about the event by their dogs' unusual behaviour. Is this a spooky canine superpower? Researchers are not yet sure exactly how dogs can sometimes sense natural disasters before they happen. Some believe that dogs may sense chemical changes in groundwater that occur before earthquakes, while others believe dogs can hear very low-frequency rumbles created by tsunamis or volcanoes. A dog's strong sense of smell might well detect changes in the air before disaster strikes. So just brace yourself next time Fido starts acting weirdly.

Another apparent superpower kicks in when dogs find their way home, even from long distances. Bizarrely, they don't need to have walked the route previously to be able to find their way back, so how do they do it? Not surprisingly, a lot of this internal GPS is down to being able to follow all manner of scent trails. Once they identify a familiar scent, they are able to follow it until they find another familiar scent, eventually making their way home.

Dogs regularly display amazing abilities and seem able to sense things in the environment when we have no idea what's going on. But, rather than having some special psychic ability or sixth sense, they more likely rely on their existing super-senses, so they can detect things long before we do. Even so, you may still be convinced your dog is paranormal!

Dogsbody

Many breeds have a physique akin to the most athletic superheroes. Is it a bird, is it a plane? No, it's a greyhound chasing a Frisbee! Be it flexibility, stamina or strength, many a dog will leave us standing.

An average dog has a skeleton with 319 bones and over 500 muscles. The most important muscle is the heart, which pumps oxygen-rich blood around the body. Large dogs' hearts beat 60–100 times per minute: small dogs' heart rate is faster, at around 100–140 beats. The skeleton protects a dog's vital organs (brain, heart, digestive system) and supports the dog's skin and muscles. Around 75% of a dog's weight is carried at the front of its body, on its shoulder joints. Unlike humans, dogs do not have collarbones; their front legs are attached to shoulderblades, which are held in place by ligaments, muscles and tendons that link them to the backbone. These 'free' forelegs give a dog great flexibility, and allow a long stride when leaping or running. The huge muscles in a dog's back legs provide the power to push it forward.

Most dogs have stamina, rather than speed: a wolf can run all day, but at only around 5 miles per hour. Dogs bred to run fast, such as greyhounds, have unusually light bone structure, huge hearts, and a higher percentage of 'fast-twitch' muscles (used for acceleration) than other dogs. Greyhounds also have a 'double-suspension gait'. At full speed, their legs are fully stretched – forwards and backwards at the same time. On the next stride, the legs fold over each other, so the back paws are in front of the forepaws.

Normal dogs move in a bewildering number of ways, depending on the size and shape of the dog's body, the length of its legs, and the speed at which it is travelling. However, all dogs run, walk, bound and leap on the tips of their toes. A dog has five toes on each front foot, including a dew-claw, which is positioned and sometimes used rather like a human thumb. Most dogs have four claws on each back foot; a few breeds have back dew-claws, as well. Claws and rough footpads (the thickest skin on a dog's body) provide grip on rough or muddy surfaces; the pads act as cushioned shock-absorbers. A small carpal pad, higher up the dog's leg, helps the dog stay stable when it is on a slope, or sliding. Dogs' feet have a thick covering of hair, and a special circulation of blood that stops flesh and skin freezing at temperatures down to −35°C.

Right at the end of our anatomical tour, the tail is one of the dog's most remarkable features. It can be straight or curled, short or long, with between 6 and 23 highly mobile vertebrae (spine-bones), and is worked by extra-strong muscles. Dogs use their tails to communicate, but tails are also important for balance, and help stabilise a dog when it is running quickly. Dogs from icy Arctic regions, such as Huskies, use their thick bushy tails to insulate and protect their eyes, nose and mouth while sleeping in freezing weather.

So, all in all, it seems the only advantage we have over dogs is our brainpower and speech. Dare we imagine how dogs may evolve further and eventually overtake us? Maybe a world ruled by canines would be far happier and no doubt a great deal of energetic fun!

Arf

Chapter 7
Quotes, jokes
& anecdotes

A man took his dog to the vet and asked for its tail to be removed. The vet asked why.
'My mother-in-law is coming to stay and there must be no indication she's welcome.'

Famous quotes

'Outside of a dog, a book is man's best friend. Inside of a dog, it's too dark to read.'

Groucho Marx

'The better I get to know men, the more I find myself loving dogs.'

Charles De Gaulle

'Did you ever walk into a room and forget why you walked in?
I think that's how dogs spend their lives.'

Sue Murphy

76

'Thorns may hurt you, men desert you, sunlight turn
to fog;
but you're never friendless ever, if you have a dog'.

Douglas Malloch

'If animals could speak, the dog would be a blundering
outspoken fellow;
but the cat would have the rare grace of never saying a
word too much.'

Mark Twain

Anonymous quotes to warm the heart

'To err is human, to forgive, canine.'

'In a perfect world, every dog would have a home and every home would have a dog.'

'He is your friend, your partner, your defender, your dog. You are his life, his love, his leader. He will be yours, faithful and true, to the last beat of his heart. You owe it to him to be worthy of such devotion.'

A shaggy dog story

A speech therapist is driving through town when he sees a sign in front of a house: 'Talking Dog For Sale.' 'This I must hear,' he laughs to himself. 'I could try teaching it to speak properly.'

He rings the doorbell and the owner tells him the dog is in the back garden. The therapist finds a Labrador Retriever sitting under a tree, reading a book called 'Dogs'.

'Hi,' says the therapist. 'Do you really talk?'

'Yep,' the dog replies. 'If I have to.'

The therapist is astonished. 'So, what have you got to say? Tell me about yourself.'

The dog looks up with a sigh and says, 'Well, I discovered that I could talk when I was pretty young – no more than a puppy, really. I needed a bit of help with p's and 'th', but they got me a good speech therapist and I even tackled a bit of French. The secret services got to hear about my gift, and in no time they had me jetting from country to country, sitting in rooms with spies and world leaders, because no one assumed a dog would be eavesdropping. I was one of their most valuable spies for eight years. But, to be honest, the jetting around really tired me out, and I knew I wasn't getting any younger, so I decided to settle down. I signed up for a job at the airport to do some undercover security stuff – listening in on suspicious characters and that sort of thing. I struck up a meaningful relationship with one of their sniffer dogs and things took off (as they often do at airports). We got married, had plenty of prize-winning puppies, settled down, and now I'm divorced, retired and apparently for sale.'

The speech therapist is speechless. He is staggered by such perfect pronunciation and articulation, so hurries indoors to ask the owner how much he wants for the dog.

'Twenty pounds.'

'Twenty pounds? That dog is exceptional. Why on earth are you selling him so cheaply?'

'Because he's nothing but a lying hound. He never did any of that stuff. He's a canine con artist. And as for all that stuff about puppies, don't believe a word of it – he's neutered!'

A random selection from The Dog Dictionary

BATH: If you find something really good to roll in, humans get jealous and they use this form of torture to get even. Be sure to shake only when next to a person or the sofa.

BUMP: The best way to get your human's attention when they are drinking a fresh cup of coffee or tea.

CHILDREN: Short humans of optimal petting height. When running, they are good to chase. If they fall down, they are comfortable to sit on.

DOG BED: Any soft, clean surface, such as the white bedspread in the guest room or the newly upholstered couch in the living room.

DROOL: A liquid that, when combined with sad eyes, forces humans to give you their food. To do this properly you must sit as close as you can and get drool on the human.

LEAD: A strap that attaches to your collar, enabling you to lead your person wherever you want him/her to go.

POSTMAN: Dinner.

SHOE: A toy with a strong smell that just has to be chewed to bits.

SNIFF: A social custom used to greet other dogs, similar to the human exchange of business cards.

THUNDER: This is a signal that the world is coming to an end. Humans remain amazingly calm during thunder, so it is necessary to warn them of the danger by trembling uncontrollably, panting, rolling your eyes wildly and howling.

WASTE BASKET: This is a dog toy filled with paper, envelopes and old wrappers. It is important to distribute its contents throughout the house before your person comes home.

WHEELIE BIN: A container that your neighbours put out once a week to test your ingenuity. You must stand on your hind legs and try to push the lid off with your nose. If you do it right you are rewarded with margarine cartons to shred, bones to chew, mouldy crusts to swallow and amazing smells to sniff and scatter for others to share.

A dog's 10 New Year resolutions:

1. I will not roll in cow dung, dead birds, fish, crabs or rabbit droppings just because I like the way they smell.

2. I will not use the sofa as a face towel.

3. I will do my best to remember that the rubbish collector is not stealing our stuff.

4. I will try not to stick my nose into someone's crotch when saying 'Hello.'

5. I will not suddenly stand straight up when I'm under the coffee table.

6. I will not wag my tail anywhere near the row of ornaments on the lower shelf.

7. I must shake the rainwater off my body before entering the house – not in the kitchen.

8. I will not sit in the middle of the living room when guests come and lick my behind.

9. I will not treat the cat like a squeaky toy... on Tuesdays.

10. I will not mistake Grandma's leg for a lamppost again.

TRUE TAILS

A true hero

Lex was the first active-duty, working military dog to be granted early retirement in order to be adopted. While working in Fallujah, Iraq with US Marine Corporal Dustin Lee, Lex was wounded in an attack that killed his handler. According to reports, despite Lex's own injuries, he refused to leave the side of Corporal Lee, and had to be dragged away to be treated by medics.

Corporal Lee's parents appealed to the US military to adopt Lex. Although not usual procedure, eventually Lex was released to the Lees. Lex, despite having over 50 pieces of shrapnel in his body, still worked as a therapy dog, visiting military veterans at hospitals and retirement homes. He died of cancer in 2012, at the age of 13.

Armed dogs in the news...

Dog sniper

In August 1999, a hunter from Bad Urach was shot dead by his own dog after he left it with a loaded gun on the back seat of his car. The 51-year-old man was found sprawled next to his car in the Black Forest. A gun barrel was pointing out of the window, and his bereaved dog was howling inside the car. The animal is presumed to have pressed the trigger with its paw. Police have ruled out foul play.

Dog shoots man

In December 2000, a New Zealand hunter was shot by his own dog, proving that canines are not always a man's best friend. Kelly Russell was tracking wild pigs with Stinky and two other dogs when the accident happened near Tokoroa on North Island. Having cornered one of his prey, Mr Russell put down his loaded shotgun – but in the ensuing commotion Stinky jumped on it, blasting a shot through the hunter's foot. Mr Russell, 30, then endured a five-hour wait for a passing car. 'There was a big bang and my leg went flying back,' the 30-year-old logger said. Maybe taking three lively dogs hunting is a mistake – a bit like shooting yourself in the foot!

Dodgy DOGgerel

My dog is a collie called Jim
And everyone jokes about him.
He's no nose, I must tell.
They ask, 'How does he smell?'
So all I can answer is, 'GRIM!'

Woof
Woof

Chapter 7
Extreme dogs

'*THEY THINK IT'S TALL ROVER. The 8 foot* towering Great Dane is in the running to be crowned the world's biggest dog. The 12-stone pooch sleeps for 22 hours each day on his adult-sized mattress.*'
(*The Sun newspaper, July 2016*)   **On his hind legs!*

*O*f course, no one will regard their own dog as just plain normal, as every pet will be special or extraordinary to its owner. Yet there will always be those dog-lovers who manage to get their extra-extraordinary dogs into the record books.

Record Size

- Lizzy, a black and white Great Dane from Florida, was the tallest dog living (female) on the planet in 2017, measuring an enormous 96.41 cm (3 ft 1.96 in) tall. Lizzy is slightly shorter than the tallest dog ever, fellow Great Dane Zeus. He lived in Michigan, USA and measured a towering 111.8 cm (3 ft 8 in).

- The smallest dog (in terms of height) recorded is a female Chihuahua called Milly, who measured 9.65 cm (3.8 in) tall in 2013 in Puerto Rico.

- The longest tail on a dog measures 76.8 cm (30.2 in), achieved by Keon, an Irish wolfhound from Belgium. He appears, along with his tail, in the 2017 edition of the *Guinness Book of World Records*.

- The world record for the longest tongue on a dog is 43 cm (17 in), belonging to Brandy, a boxer from Michigan, USA. He died in 2002.

- The largest wild dog of all time was Hayden's bone-crushing dog (Epicyon haydeni). Estimated to weigh up to 170 kg (374.8 lb), it was about the size of a modern lion and it lived during the mid-late Miocene epoch (20 – 5 million years ago) in North America.

Biggest family

The largest litter of puppies recorded was 24, all born to Tia, a Neopolitan mastiff in 2004, in the UK. 20 of the puppies survived.

Extreme random achievements of dogdom

- The fastest 100 metre dash on a skateboard by a dog was 19.65 seconds, achieved by Jumpy the dog (USA) on the set of 'Officially Amazing' in California, USA in 2013.

- The loudest bark by a dog measured 113.1 dB and was produced by golden retriever Charlie, in Australia during the Purina Bark in the Park event in Adelaide, 2012. Not the place to go for a quiet stroll in the park!

- A Japanese dog called Purin won her second world record, by travelling 10 metres on a large ball, in just 11.9 seconds. She added it to her other world record, from 2015, when she proved her great paw-eye coordination by catching 14 balls in one minute.

- The most tricks performed by a dog in one minute were 32, achieved by Smurf in Hertfordshire, UK, in 2015. Some of the tricks Smurf performed included walking on his back paws, rolling over, limping, begging and bowing.

Extreme dogs

- The fastest time to pop 100 balloons by a dog is 39.08 seconds and was achieved by Twinkie, a Jack Russell in the USA in 2014. Twinkie's mother, Anastasia, previously held this record. A family bursting with energy.

- The most dogs balancing a treat on their nose is 109, achieved by The Link Management Ltd (Hong Kong), in 2014. Previous records set here were for the largest dog obedience lesson, the most people brushing dogs' teeth simultaneously and the largest dog grooming lesson. Well, someone's got to do it!

And finally...

The oldest known age for a dog was 29 years 5 months for an Australian cattle-dog named Bluey who lived from 1910 to 1939. Most dogs live for 8–15 years, and authentic records of dogs living over 20 years are rare and generally involve the smaller breeds.

Glossary

Alexander the Great an ancient king of Macedon who conquered a large part of the world, including Egypt, Syria, Persia and Mesopotamia.

anatomical relating to the structure of a living organism.

anthropomorphic when human behaviour or characteristics are projected onto animals or objects.

cynophobia the fear of dogs.

hormone substances transported around the body via blood and other fluids which regulate the function and operation of specific cells and tissues.

Middle Ages the period in European history from the fall of the Western Roman Empire until the fall of Constantinople in 1453.

Neolithic the latter part of the Stone Age era, when polished or ground stone tools became prevalent.

olfactory related to the sense of smell.

portent a sign or omen that a significant event is about to occur.

primates an order of mammals, including monkeys, apes and humans, distinguished by having hands, hand-like feet and forward-facing eyes.

primordial the earliest stage of biological development.

Roman empire the empire centred around the city of Rome and established in 27 BC that conquered territories across Europe, North Africa and the Middle East.

sentimentality an excessive and cloying degree of tenderness or emotion.

ultraviolet light part of the spectrum of light that is not visible to the human eye.

Index